Shoes Along the Highway

By Maureen Brady Johnson

Single copies of plays are sold for reading purposes only. The copying or duplicating of a play, or any part of play, by hand or by any other process, is an infringement of the copyright. Such infringement will be vigorously prosecuted

Baker's Plays
c/o Samuel French, Inc.
45 West 25 Street
New York, NY 10010
bakersplays.com

NOTICE

This book is offered for sale at the price quoted only on the understanding that, if any additional copies of the whole or any part are necessary for its production, such additional copies will be purchased. The attention of all purchasers is directed to the following: This work is protected under the copyright laws of the United States of America, in the British Empire, including the Dominion of Canada, and all other countries adhering to the Universal Copyright Convention. Violations of the Copyright Law are punishable by fine or imprisonment, or both. The copying or duplication of this work or any part of this work, by hand or by any process, is an infringement of the copyright and will be vigorously prosecuted.

This play may not be produced by amateurs or professionals for public or private performance without first submitting application for performing rights. Royalties are due on all performances whether for charity or gain, or whether admission is charged or not Since performance of this play without the payment of the royalty fee renders anybody participating liable to severe penalties imposed by the law, anybody acting in this play should be sure, before doing so, that the royalty fee has been paid. Professional rights, reading rights, radio broadcasting, television and all mechanical rights, etc. are strictly reserved. Application for performing rights should be made directly to BAKER'S PLAYS.

No one shall commit or authorize any act or omission by which the copyright of, or the right to copyright, this play may be impaired. No one shall make any changes in this play for the purpose of production.

Publication of this play does not imply availability for performance. Both amateurs and professionals considering a production are strongly advised in their own interest to apply to Baker's Plays for written permission before starting rehearsals, advertising, or booking a theatre.

Whenever the play is produced, the author's name must be carried in all publicity, advertising and programs. Also, the following notice must appear on all printed programs, "Produced by special arrangement with Baker's Plays."

Licensing fees for *SHOES ALONG THE HIGHWAY* is based on a per performance rate and payable one week in advance of the production. Please consult the Baker's Plays website at www.bakersplays.com or our current print catalogue for up to date licensing fee information.

Copyright © 2008 by Maureen Brady Johnson
Made in U.S.A. All rights reserved.

SHOES ALONG THE HIGHWAY
ISBN 978-0-87440-293-3   # 1788-B

SHOES ALONG THE HIGHWAY was first performed by students at Lake Ridge Academy, North Ridgeville, Ohio on June 2, 2004 with the following cast:

JEREMY . . . . Isaac Jilbert
HIS MOM . . . . Samantha Fay
LENORE . . . . Erica Lasky
NORBERT . . . . Aiden Mullaney
POLICEWOMAN . . . . Kendal Szulewski-Francis
HANK . . . . Andy Milluzzi
JANICE . . . . Alexandra Hansen
MR. THOMAS . . . . Matthew Nahorn
MR. HIGHTOWER . . . . Zachary Sweebe
MRS. GRANT . . . . Brooke Arthur-Mensah
CLARE . . . . Diane Colley

Assistant to the Director: Kara Walsh
Stage Manager: Kendal Szulewski-Francis
Tech: Andy Milluzzi

CHARACTERS

JEREMY: A high school senior
HIS MOM: An art professor
LENORE: Jeremy's sister, a high school freshman
NORBERT: Jeremy's brother, a fifth grader
A POLICEMAN or **POLICEWOMAN**
HANK: a football player
JANICE: Hank's girlfriend
MR. THOMAS: the dean of discipline/assistant principal
MR/MRS. HIGHTOWER: substitute teacher…retired librarian
MR/MRS. GRANT: the art teacher
CLARE: Jeremy's friend

NOTE: The play can be performed with a full cast (11) or you can double up on the parts with some performers taking on multiple roles (8). If you decide to do this, the costumes should be easy to change between scenes; i.e., A hat, sunglasses and coat for the POLICEMAN, a team jacket for HANK.

Possible doubling could be:
POLICEMAN/MR. THOMAS
HANK/MR. HIGHTOWER
LENORE/JANICE
Gender can also be changed to fit the cast when appropriate.

SETTING

The set is very simple, the suggestion of a place... the car (four chairs or stools), the school hallway (a large garbage can), the art room, (a table, four stools, an easel, a CD player), the gallery (the stools from the art room with the pictures hanging above). The set changes should be made quickly and quietly by the cast during Jeremy's monologues. Using many of the same set pieces for every scene really speeds up the amount of time between scenes and doesn't interrupt the flow of the play. Using background music can also help the scene changes run smoothly.

SET PLOT

The poster size photos of the shoes are hung upstage. During the opening, the museum scene and the closing scenes they should be lit.

Scene One: Jeremy onstage with bag of shoes
Scene Two: Four chairs or stools arranged to resemble car seats
Scene Three: A large garbage can
Scene Four: The Art room. A small table, an easel with a large canvas, 2 or 3 stools, a CD player
Scene Five: The Art room
Scene Six: The Art museum. Three stools with the three shoes placed on them.
Scene Seven: The Art room.
Scene Eight: Jeremy in the same position as scene one.

My family, Mark, Erin, Allison, Juliet and Sean

At Rise:

Music cue.

(JEREMY, stands stage right as the lights come up on him. HE has a camera on a strap around his neck and is holding a brown paper bag. HE opens the bag and dumps its contents onto the stage. Six shoes, none of them matching, all of them old and weathered, fall to the floor. One of the shoes must be a child's tennis shoe with laces.)

(As HE speaks, the lights come up onstage revealing three large photographs hung above the stage, pictures of single shoes on the highway. One photo should be of the child's tennis shoe with laces, the other two of any of the shoes in the bag.)

JEREMY. *(Addressing the audience, HE indicates the pile of shoes on the floor)*

What do you see here? Shoes? Yeah, you're right.

(HE picks up a shoe, describing it to the audience)

A work boot. A dress shoe. A kid's sneaker.

They're all over the place. Just one shoe. On the side of the road. I started picking them up on my trip here from California, my *real* home.

(Pause)

See, my mom's an art history professor. My dad's a photographer…was a photographer. He died last year.

Suddenly, my mom needed to go home.

So, she took us halfway around the world to this little town in Ohio where she grew up. She got a job teaching at the college.

It's *her* home, not mine.

(HE indicates the camera)

I'm a photographer. Like my dad. This is his camera.

(Pause)

I see pictures everywhere. And behind every picture, there's a story. I can't stop seeing the pictures and trying to figure out the stories. I guess I'm like my dad, trying to tell the stories by freezing time in a picture.

*(Pause as **HE** picks up all but two of the shoes and puts them back in the bag. **HE** leaves two shoes onstage. Four chairs/stools brought onstage. They are set up to look like a car, front seat and back.)*

I like looking out the window on long trips. And this trip was really long. And sad. We were all together but very much alone, each of us dealing with the pictures in our head.

(Pause)

I think that's why my mom stopped when I asked to take a picture of the shoe. She wouldn't have given it a second thought on any other trip; too dangerous. But this time, she stopped.

*(Sound of a car driving. **MOM** enters, sits in the front seat. **LENORE** and **NORBERT** sit in the back seats. **JEREMY** takes the bag of shoes and sits in the front next to his **MOM**. **LENORE** and **NORBERT** are wearing headphones singing loudly to their music. The songs they are singing are very different.)*

MOM. *(tries to get **LENORE** and **NORBERT**'s attention)*
Hey. Hey, you two! We had a rule. No singing when you're wearing headphones. I can't drive with all the noise.

LENORE & NORBERT. Sorry, Mom.

*(**THEY** continue to listen to their music)*

MOM. I can't wait to show you the art museum. I used to walk over there and sit in the gallery and sketch. You guys are gonna love it.

(Silence)

And there's a five and dime on Main Street, a real five and dime. At least, I think it's still there. They had penny candy. Can you imagine? Candy for a penny.

(Silence)

And the people are so nice. When they pass you on the street, they say "Hi, there."...complete strangers say, "Hi, there." I know you're gonna love it.

(Silence)

Is anyone listening to me? Jeremy?

JEREMY. Yeah, Mom. Art museum, five and dime, nice people who talk to strangers...Mom, we just passed a shoe. If we see another one, can you stop and let me take a picture?

MOM. Are you crazy? You'll get killed.

JEREMY. There's no one on the road. Look, I'll jump out, snap the picture and jump back in the car.

MOM. I think there's a law against it. I don't need a policeman stopping me now.

JEREMY. Mom, you've been going 75 on a 65 road for an hour now.

MOM. You're too smart for your own good, y'know that?

JEREMY. Look, there's one up ahead.

MOM. I must be out of my mind.

*(**SHE** mimes pulling over and stopping the car. **LENORE** and **NORBERT**, in the back seat, take off their earphones)*

LENORE. Why are we stopping? Are we getting something to eat?

NORBERT. Yeah, I'm hungry. Let's go to McDonalds.

LENORE. No. I want Subway.

NORBERT. No. We went to Subway yesterday.

LENORE. But Subway's good for you, right, Mom?

NORBERT. No...Pizza Hut or Chinese. I love Chinese. Can I eat with chopsticks, Mom? Please?

MOM. We are not stopping for food. Jeremy is taking a picture of a shoe.

LENORE. Gross.

NORBERT. Cool! Can I get out and see it.

MOM. No. Stay right where you are. Jeremy, hop out and shoot fast.

(**JEREMY** *hops out of the car and takes a picture of one of the shoes that was left onstage.* **HE** *picks up the shoe and brings it back to the car.*)

MOM. *(continuing)* You guys are gonna love Ohio. Did I tell you that the house I grew up in is on Apple Blossom Drive? I wonder what it looks like now.

LENORE. Mom, Jeremy picked up the shoe! He's touching it! No, he's bringing that filthy shoe back to the car. Oh my God!

NORBERT. Can I see it?

MOM. Jeremy, hurry up! There's a truck coming.

(**JEREMY** *hops back into the car.* **MOM** *pulls the car back onto the road.*)

NORBERT. Can I touch it?

JEREMY. No.

MOM. Why did you pick up the shoe?

JEREMY. I don't know. Seemed like I should.

LENORE. There's bugs all over it! Oh my God, there's something moving inside of it!

(**JEREMY** *knocks the contents of the shoe out the window*)

NORBERT. How come you let HIM touch it, Mom? I mean, I've been good. I've stayed on my side of the car...I haven't bugged Lenore...Let me touch the shoe.

MOM. Norbert, Stop. Jeremy, I don't want it in the car if it's got bugs.

JEREMY. I cleaned it out. C'mon, let me keep it. It's FOUND art, Mom.

LENORE. If that shoe stays, I'm walking to Ohio. It's not art. It's garbage.

JEREMY. Lenore, you were born thinking of one thing, boys.

LENORE. I'm almost a freshman. That's what I'm supposed to think about. At least I don't hide behind a camera.

NORBERT. Oooo…burn!

MOM. Cut it out! Put the shoe in the bag.

(**JEREMY** *does*)

NORBERT. Can I put my hand in the bag and touch it?

JEREMY. No, Norby. You'll wreck it.

NORBERT. How can I wreck a dirty old shoe?

JEREMY. It's falling apart. One of the straps broke off when I picked it up.

LENORE. Oh my God! I can hear it now. "Oh that's Lenore. She drove from California with her family and a trashy, old shoe they found along the highway. I'll never make any friends."

JEREMY. Mom, there's another one. Pull over.

LENORE. Don't do it, Mom!

(**MOM** *pulls the car over.* **JEREMY** *jumps out and takes another picture, picks up the shoe and hops back into the car. While* **JEREMY** *is out of the car,* **NORBERT** *picks up the brown paper bag, opens it, sticks his hand in it and touches the shoe.*)

LENORE. Get your hand out of that bag, Norby.

NORBERT. You are not the boss of me, Lenny.

LENORE. I'm getting out of here.

(**SHE** *gets out of the car.* **MOM** *follows her and tries to bring her back to the car.*)

MOM. Lenny, get back in the car.

LENORE. My name is not Lenny. It's Lenore. And I am not going to Ohio with a bunch of dirty shoes. In fact, I'm not going to Ohio at all.

(SHE starts to walk away)

MOM. Get inside the car. We're both going to get killed out here.

LENORE. I don't care.

MOM. Well, I do. We'll talk *inside* the car!

LENORE. Oh. *Now* you want to talk about it.

MOM. What's that supposed to mean?

LENORE. All you've talked about the whole trip is how much *you* want to go home. It's YOUR home we're going to, Mom. *Our* home is in California. Did you ever ask us what we wanted to do? Did you ever think what this move would do to us?

MOM. I thought you wanted to move.

LENORE. You told us we were moving.

JEREMY. *(Returning to the car)* Norby give me the bag.

NORBERT. Let me touch the shoe.

LENORE. I am not getting in the car.

JEREMY. Give me the bag!

NORBERT. MOM!!!!

(The LOUD sound of a truck horn. MOM and LENORE immediately get into the car. THEY all take a deep breath.)

MOM. That was close.

JEREMY. Lenny?

LENORE. My name is Lenore!

NORBERT. I touched it.

LENORE. Norby!

NORBERT. I touched it with this finger, Lenny.

(HE threatens to touch HER with the finger)

LENORE. MOM!

JEREMY. Norby, leave her alone and give me the bag!

(JEREMY tries to grab the bag from NORBERT)

MOM. CUT IT OUT…ALL OF YOU!

(Silence)

Jeremy, put the shoe in the bag, put the bag under the seat, far away from Lenny,

*(**LENNY** gives her mom an exasperated look)*

MOM. Norbert, you can see the shoes,

NORBERT. Yes!

MOM. But not until we get to Ohio and they're cleaned up.

NORBERT. Aw, man.

MOM. Lenore, no one in this car will tell any of your new friends about the shoes. Everyone repeat after me, We Won't Tell.

ALL. We won't tell.

MOM. *(takes a deep, sad breath)* Listen....I'm sorry...I really screwed up. I thought I was doing the right thing. I thought if we got away it would be easier. Obviously, I was wrong. But here we are and ...look...

(Pause)

I can't get through this without you.

(Sound of a police siren)

Oh, my God. No one speaks until spoken to.

*(A **POLICEMAN** walks on stage left. Leans over to talk to **MOM**.)*

POLICEMAN. Good morning.

MOM. Good morning, Officer.

POLICEMAN. Is everything all right?

MOM. Yes, officer. Just having a family discussion.

POLICEMAN. Well, there's a rest stop about 3 miles up the road. It might be safer to have that family discussion there.

MOM. Yes, sir. We will.

POLICEMAN. You kids better buckle up back there.

LENORE & NORBERT. Yes, sir.

POLICEMAN. Do you need help getting back on the highway?

MOM. No, sir.

POLICEMAN. Well, be careful, now. And keep those seatbelts on.

*(**POLICEMAN** exits)*

MOM. Yes, sir. We will.

*(There is complete silence in the car as **MOM** starts up the car and gets back on the highway.)*

NORBERT. Mom, Can you hurry? I gotta go really bad.

*(Music cue. **JEREMY** steps down right with the bag of shoes in his hands. The performers take their chairs/stools offstage. The sound of a school bell is heard. Garbage can is brought onstage during Jeremy's speech)*

JEREMY. New school. Big school. Huge, public school. A lot bigger than my old school. Lots of kids trying to be popular here. I didn't care about being popular. I stayed out of their way…tried to blend in…lurk in the shadows…but as the new kid I knew I couldn't hide forever. I just hoped I'd graduate in one piece.

*(**JANICE** and **HANK** enter right and bump into **JEREMY**. The shoes fall out of the bag onto the floor. **JANICE** and **HANK** laugh. **JEREMY** begins to pick up the shoes.)*

HANK. Hey. What's with the shoes?

JANICE. Yeah. What's with the shoes?

*(Silently, **JEREMY** puts the shoes, except one, in the bag)*

HANK. I'm talking to you.

JANICE. Yeah. He's talking to you.

HANK. You some kind of weirdo? Some kind of freak?

JANICE. Yeah. Weirdo? Freak?

HANK. Hey! You deaf? What's with the bag of crap?

*(As **HANK** speaks **HE** walks over and steps on the kid's tennis shoe to keep **JEREMY** from picking it up. **JEREMY** realizes that **HE** is going to have to talk to **HANK**. **MR. THOMAS**, assistant principal, enters, unobserved)*

JEREMY. Art Project.

HANK. *(Picking up the shoe)* You're gonna use this garbage for an Art Project? What do you see here, Janice? Is this Art?

JANICE. Eeeewww! It smells bad.

> *(**SHE** takes out a mirror to check her make-up and hair)*

HANK. Sure looks like a bunch of garbage to me. What do you think Janice? Should I throw this away?

> *(**JANICE** is still looking at herself in the mirror. **HANK** goes to throw the shoe in the garbage can.)*

JEREMY. It's not garbage. Give me my shoe.

HANK. "Give me my shoe" This iddy, biddy kiddy's shoe is yours?

JEREMY. It's my property. Give it back.

HANK. How can you fit your big, fat foot in this iddy, biddy shoe?

JEREMY. *(Quietly)* The same way you fit your big, fat head into….

JANICE. *(Interrupting)* Hey, that's a camera right?

JEREMY. I'm surprised you recognize it.

JANICE. Take my picture! Hank, make him take my picture.

HANK. OK, Camera boy. Take a picture of me throwing your teeny, tiny shoe away. Janice, get over here.

JANICE. No. It smells bad. I want a picture of me and you.

JEREMY. Give me my shoe.

HANK. Janice, I said get over here. NOW.

> *(**JANICE** hurries to his side, staying away from the dangling shoe)*

> Take the picture. And then maybe I'll let you fish it out of the trash after I bury it.

MR. THOMAS. What's going on here?

HANK. *(Suddenly polite)* Janice and I were just trying to clean up the halls. Isn't that right Janice?

JANICE. Yes, Mr. Thomas. We're just trying to clean up the halls.

MR. THOMAS. Well, then I'll see you both after school tonight and you can help the custodian.

HANK. But, Mr. Thomas, I have a big scrimmage tonight.

MR. THOMAS. Then I guess they'll just have to play without you. Get to class.

(**HANK** *leaves SR throwing the shoe at* **JEREMY**'s *feet.* **JANICE** *follows* **HANK**)

MR. THOMAS (CONT.) You're new, aren't you?

JEREMY. *(Putting the child's shoe into his bag)* Yes, sir.

MR. THOMAS. Jeremy, right?

JEREMY. Yes.

MR. THOMAS. Do you know who I am?

JEREMY. Yes. Mr. Thomas. Assistant Principal. Dean of Discipline.

MR. THOMAS. They call me Mr. T for short. Do you know who Mr. T is?

JEREMY. Yes, sir. I do.

MR. THOMAS. You do? Who is Mr. T?

JEREMY. He's a member of the A-team and he gets people out of trouble.

MR. THOMAS. Why, yes. That's correct. *(Kindly)* Look, Jeremy. I don't like trouble. Don't give me any trouble. OK?

JEREMY. I won't, sir.

(**MR. THOMAS** *exits. Music cue.* **JEREMY** *takes the bag of shoes and moves downstage. The set is changed while he speaks. A small table and the stools are moved onstage. A boom box sits on the table. An easel with a large canvas is moved onstage.* **CLARE** *sits behind the easel, unseen by the audience.*)

JEREMY. At my old school, if you were looking for me, you'd find me in the art room. At my new school, it was the only place that I kind of felt at home.

But, the new art teacher was not like my old art teacher.

Mr. Hightower. I couldn't believe this guy. He spoke through his nose, like this...

*(**JEREMY** imitates **MR. HIGHTOWER**. The actor who plays **HIGHTOWER** should use the same quirky character traits as **JEREMY**)*

"Senior artists, may I have your attention? There will be a Senior Art Show exhibited at the college's art museum. The winning pieces will go on to New York and you will be eligible for a generous scholarship to attend some of the most prestigious art schools in the country."

He would also pace and talk at the same time.

*(**JEREMY** imitates Mr Hightower by pacing)*

"You must install your pieces at the museum after school the day before the show. Your craftsmanship must be impeccable and every piece must be labeled correctly. Each senior must attend the opening reception when the judges will bestow the gold key awards."

And, when he was really nervous, he would look at the walls, the ceiling, out the window, but never at you.

*(**JEREMY** imitates Mr Hightower with all the quirks)*

"The medium you use must be declared and a description of your artwork written up and submitted to be approved by the department head. Get to work on your proposals. Good luck."

I wanted to use the shoes with the photographs but I didn't know how to do it. So, I took my shoes and the photographs to the art room to ask Mr. Hightower about it.

*(**MR. HIGHTOWER** enters stage right)*

JEREMY. Mr. Hightower, I need your help.

MR. HIGHTOWER. Well, that's why I'm here... to help you.

JEREMY. I took these photographs of shoes...

MR. HIGHTOWER. Oil.

JEREMY. What?

MR. HIGHTOWER. Oil. I think you should stick to oil.

JEREMY. Oil?

MR. HIGHTOWER. Perhaps I am not making myself clear. I think you should do an oil painting of the shoes.

JEREMY. I don't want to do a painting. I want to use the photographs and make some kind of connection with the real shoes.

MR. HIGHTOWER. *(Patronizing)* Jeremy. Jeremy. Oh, Jeremy.

(Pause)

It is Jeremy, isn't it?

JEREMY. Yes. It's Jeremy.

MR. HIGHTOWER. From the sunny state of California? Right?

JEREMY. Yeah.

MR. HIGHTOWER. Maybe in *California* photography is considered an art but *here* it is considered a hobby.

JEREMY. Mr. Hightower, photography is considered an art everywhere. Margaret Bourke-White, Edward Steichen, Ansel Adams…they're all artists.

MR. HIGHTOWER. Snapping a picture is not art. Painting and drawing are *real* art forms.

JEREMY. With all due respect, Mr. Hightower, these photographs are real art. They challenge an audience. A person looking at one of these photos asks, "How did a single shoe end up on the highway?"

MR. HIGHTOWER. Some petulant child probably threw it out the window of a car.

JEREMY. Yeah. But there's more to it than that. Here, look at this picture. A red dress shoe. What the heck happened here? Did some girl go to her prom with only one shoe? These photos demand a response from their audience. They demand that they think.

MR. HIGHTOWER. Think? What about?

JEREMY. About loneliness and rejection. Growing old and getting tossed out. About losing something or someone.

MR. HIGHTOWER. The accepted medium of great art is and always has been *oil*. Do a nice painting of one of your shoes and be done with it.

JEREMY. I don't want to do something NICE. NICE equals NUMB. I want my audience to think.

MR. HIGHTOWER. Jeremy! Listen. You can write up your proposal just like the rest of the students and we'll see if it gets accepted.

JEREMY. But I need help with my proposal. That's why I came to you.

MR. HIGHTOWER. And that's why I'm here …to help you. But, not at this moment. I'm on my way to a meeting and I have been asked to take notes.

(**HE** *is obviously thrilled with this honor.* **HE** *exits.* **JEREMY** *collects the shoes and puts them into the bag.*)

CLARE. *(From behind the easel)* Don't give up.

JEREMY. *(Startled to hear a voice)* Whoa. I thought I was the only one in here. What'd you say?

CLARE. *(Coming out a bit from behind the easel)* Sorry. I said don't give up.

JEREMY. On my proposal, my shoes or my theory on art?

CLARE. All of the above.

(*She goes back behind the easel*)

JEREMY. *(keeps packing up the shoes)* Thanks for the advice. Are you a senior?

CLARE. Yep.

JEREMY. I haven't seen you in class.

CLARE. I'm an "Independent Study." I come in during my free time.

JEREMY. ALL your free time?

CLARE. Yep.

JEREMY. What about your friends?

CLARE. Don't have many. Where did you take the photos?

JEREMY. Colorado, Illinois, Indiana. Some right outside of town.

CLARE. Right outside of town?

JEREMY. Yeah.

CLARE. Can I see them?

JEREMY. Can see your painting?

CLARE. Nope. Not quite ready yet.

JEREMY. When will you be ready?

CLARE. Depends on you.

JEREMY. Me?

CLARE. Yeah. I've been watching you.

JEREMY. Really? From behind that easel?

CLARE. You'd be surprised what you can learn from behind an easel..

JEREMY. What have you learned?

CLARE. Well, let's see. Your name is Jeremy. *(Imitating Hightower)* It is Jeremy, isn't it?

JEREMY. *(He gets the joke)* Yes. It's Jeremy.

CLARE. OK. Jeremy: from California, passionate about photography, although I haven't figured that out yet.

JEREMY. My dad. He gave me a camera when I was six. We'd get up early Sunday mornings. Sometimes we'd be gone all day. He'd always make toasted peanut butter and honey sandwiches when we got back.

CLARE. Love them with bananas.

JEREMY. No way!

CLARE. Yes, way. So, do you and your dad still go out on Sundays?

JEREMY. Not any more. My dad died last year and my mom moved us here. It's her hometown.

CLARE. Sorry. I didn't know.

JEREMY. That's OK. You couldn't know. I haven't told anyone.

CLARE. Is that his camera?

JEREMY. Yeah. It's old. Nothing fancy, but it gets some great shots. I was hopping in and out of the car all the way from California every time I saw a shoe, taking pictures. Now I don't know what to do with them.

CLARE. Why don't you show them to the real art teacher?

JEREMY. What do you mean? Isn't Hightower…?

CLARE. Nope. The real art teacher is Mrs. Grant. She's in Italy taking classes in art restoration. She'll be back in a few days.

JEREMY. Then who's Hightower?

CLARE. He's a sub. Retired librarian. Couldn't you tell?

JEREMY. Oh, yeah. Yeah.

(Short pause)

No. Not really. I just thought he was a Midwest version of an art teacher.

CLARE. Oh, yeah? I hope I'm not a Midwest version of an artist.

JEREMY. Well, if you let me take a peek at your painting, I could tell you.

CLARE. No. Not yet.

JEREMY. Ok. Well, I gotta pick up my little brother…

CLARE. *(From behind the easel)* See you around, Jeremy, photographer, consumer of peanut butter and honey sandwiches. See, I'm learning.

JEREMY. Hey. I never got your name.

CLARE. *(sticks her head out from behind the easel)* Clare.

JEREMY. Clare?

CLARE. My mom named me after an Art Garfunkle song.

JEREMY. Angel Clare?

CLARE. Wow. Not many people know that, Jeremy: photographer, consumer of PBH's and totally intriguing person. I'll see you around.

(She disappears behind the easel)

JEREMY. Yeah. See you around.

(The lights dim. **CLARE** *exits. The set remains the same. To Audience)*

I bet I know what you're thinking. Angel Clare. She's gonna swoop into my life and make everything all right. You're forgetting that there are many different kinds of Angels. There's those little baby angels called Cherubs and there's the Angel of Death. You're also thinking that, for a kid, I know a lot about angels. Hey, I'm an intriguing personality.

*(***JEREMY*** starts to take the shoes out of the bag and lay them on top of the table.)*

So, a week goes by and my contest proposal is still not written and the deadline's Friday. I really need the money for college. The first chance I get, I ask the real art teacher about the shoes.

*(***MRS. GRANT*** walks into the Art room.* **SHE** *crosses to the table where* **JEREMY** *has just finished laying out the shoes. During this scene* **MRS. GRANT** *examines the shoes.)*

MRS. GRANT. That's quite a collection.

JEREMY. I have pictures to match.

MRS. GRANT. Where did you find all of these?

JEREMY. On the side of the road. I want to use them with the photos but I'm not quite sure how to do it.

MRS. GRANT. Can I see the photos?

JEREMY. Sure.

*(***HE** *gives* **HER** *the pictures.* **SHE** *looks at them.)*

Some of them aren't as good as others. I had to shoot fast. There was a lot of traffic on some of the roads.

MRS. GRANT. *(pulls out three of the pictures)* These three are the best. Use Photoshop to clean them up.

JEREMY. I want to use the shoes, too.

MRS. GRANT. Why?

JEREMY. Reality meets Art. It forces people to think. Drivers were zooming by these shoes, never giving them a thought. I want to force them to face the reality, to question how a single shoe ends up on a highway.

MRS. GRANT. Yeah. I just saw one riding the baggage return when I came back from Italy. One shoe. Going round and round. I thought, "What the heck…"

(**SHE** *picks up the red dress shoe*)

Where did you find this?

JEREMY. On an entrance ramp in Indiana. It was pretty messed up when I found it.

MRS. GRANT. And this kid's shoe?

JEREMY. I actually found that one outside of town.

MRS. GRANT. Makes you wonder what the heck happened before the shoe hit the pavement.

(**SHE** *picks up another shoe*)

How about putting the shoes on pedestals? Enlarge these three photographs and hang them above the shoes.

JEREMY. Yeah. Good idea. They'll look at the shoe and think "What the heck?" Then they'll look at the photo, look at the shoe again and ask, "How did that shoe get there?"

MRS. GRANT. Jeremy, you're taking a big risk here.

JEREMY. How's that?

MRS. GRANT. This is pretty unusual. The judges may not see it the same way. You may not win anything.

JEREMY. Yeah. I thought about that. The whole time I've been here, most people have been saying these shoes are garbage. But, I'm gonna do it. My Dad always said, "Let the work speak for itself."

MRS. GRANT. Smart man.

JEREMY. Yeah.

MRS. GRANT. Well, sounds like this is a done deal. Should I give the museum a call and find out about the pedestals?

JEREMY. Yeah. Thanks, Mrs. Grant.

MRS. GRANT. No problem.

(Classical music cue)

JEREMY. I got the photos enlarged and hung, cleaned up the shoes a bit, and helped with the installation. I didn't see Clare for weeks. She always seemed to be somewhere else when I was in the art room.

(**JEREMY** *puts all of the shoes except the three he is using for the exhibit back into the bag. The art room is struck and the stage changes to the "gallery."* **JEREMY** *sets up the exhibit.* **HE** *walks around and places the shoes that match the hanging photographs on the pedestals.*)

The senior show was a bigger deal than I thought it would be. Lots of people came to the museum on the night of the opening; students, parents, college professors and people who lived on farms outside of town.

(The museum scene is a pantomime. As **JEREMY** *speaks, the performers silently move through the action.* **MR. THOMAS** *and* **MR. HIGHTOWER** *enter first.)*

Some people got it...

(**MR. THOMAS** *likes what he sees*)

and some people didn't...

(**MR. HIGHTOWER** *doesn't*)

(**HANK** *and* **JANICE** *enter*)

Some people thought it was just garbage.

(**THEY** *obviously don't understand the artwork.*)

But I was convinced to let the art speak for itself.

(**LENORE** *enters*)

Some people were preoccupied with other things and didn't take the time to think.

(**SHE** *sees some friends offstage and waves to them and rushes off to join them.*)

(**MOM** *and* **NORBERT** *enter.* **NORBERT** *tries to touch the shoes when* **MOM** *isn't looking.* **HE** *fails with the first two but succeeds with the last shoe.* **MOM** *gives* **JEREMY** *a pat on the back.*)

Some people would have loved anything I did. But a lot of people took the time to think and wonder about the story behind the shoe.

(**CLARE** *walks into the museum, sees the child's shoe, stops for a moment and then immediately walks out.* **JEREMY** *tries to catch* **CLARE***'s attention.* **HE** *is puzzled that she leaves so quickly.* **MRS. GRANT** *enters*)

Mrs. Grant told me she thought it was a very creative and unusual approach. She still worried that the judges wouldn't consider it for an award.

(**EVERYONE** *leaves.* **JEREMY** *collects the shoes from the pedestals*)

But by the end of the evening, my artwork had a gold key for best of show.

(**JEREMY** *moves downstage and continues to speak while the set is being changed back to the art room. The stools and table are set up and the easel is brought onstage. The CD player and a brown box are placed on the table.*)

You might think that this is the happy ending of my story. Don't get me wrong, "New Kid in Town Makes Good" is a great ending. Like some kind of a fairytale. But my life was not a fairytale.

(*Pause*)

The Monday following the show, I had to pack up my pictures and the shoes for the trip to New York, so I stayed after school. I was hoping to catch Clare in the art room to congratulate her. One of her paintings was also going to New York. It was powerful. But it wasn't the one she was working on in the art room. She still wasn't sharing that one.

(**MRS. GRANT** *enters.* **JEREMY** *begins to put the shoes into the box*)

MRS. GRANT. Feeling good, Mr. Gold Key Winner?

JEREMY. Yeah. I just hope the judges in New York see it the same way.

MRS. GRANT. There's a good chance they will. Make sure all the shoes are packed up. Everything has to go. Do you need any more packing stuff? I've got a ton of those packing peanuts and some bubble wrap.

JEREMY. I don't need the peanuts, but I could sure use the bubble wrap.

MRS. GRANT. OK. I'll get it for you. I've got to dig it out of the back room. I'll be a minute.

(SHE exits)

JEREMY. OK. Thanks.

(CLARE walks in Stage Right. SHE walks past JEREMY without saying a word. SHE walks over to a boom box, punches play and cranks up the volume. She crosses to her easel and begins to paint.)

JEREMY. *(Shouting over the music)* Hey. Where've you been?

(CLARE doesn't answer. JEREMY goes to the boom box and puts it on pause.)

Hey. Clare. I asked you where you've been.

CLARE. Around. Could you put the music back on?

JEREMY. Congratulations on your gold key. Your painting was awesome.

CLARE. Look, I really need the music to work.

JEREMY. Why didn't you enter the one you've been working on?

CLARE. I'm not ready to show it to just anyone. Could you turn the music back on?

JEREMY. Are you mad at me?

CLARE. No. I want to work.

JEREMY. OK.

(HE turns the music on. HE begins to pack up the shoes. Shouting over the music, JEREMY asks...)

Hey, Clare, did you see my exhibit? What did you think of my shoes?

CLARE. *(goes to boom box and turns the music off.)* Are those the shoes that you used?

JEREMY. Yeah.

CLARE. Give me the kid's shoe.

JEREMY. OK. Here.

> (**HE** *gives her the kid's shoe. The shoelaces should be untied.* **SHE** *looks inside the shoe*)

CLARE. My God. This is hers. These are her initials.

> (**MRS. GRANT** *enters and listens to their conversation*)

JEREMY. Whose initials?

CLARE. My sister's.

JEREMY. What's your sister's shoe doing out on the road?

MRS. GRANT. Are you sure?

CLARE. Yeah. I'm sure. When they brought her in, she was only wearing one shoe.

> (*Pause*)

> Jeremy. I want this shoe.

JEREMY. What? Why? I have to send it to New York.

CLARE. No, it's not going to New York. I don't want people gawking at it.

JEREMY. What?

MRS. GRANT. Clare, why didn't you say something before this?

CLARE. I wasn't sure. Now I know. It's hers.

JEREMY. Would somebody please tell me what's going on?

MRS. GRANT. Clare's sister was killed outside of town. Drunk driver.

CLARE. This is her shoe.

> (*Pause*)

> Why did you pick up this shoe?

JEREMY. I thought it had a story.

CLARE. *(Short pause. Looking at the shoe)* The day she died, just before she left the house, she asked me to help her tie her shoes. I said, "Tie them yourself." She said she couldn't and I told her to grow up.

That was the very, last thing I said to her… "Grow Up"

MRS. GRANT. You didn't know what was going to happen.

JEREMY. I'm sorry. If I had known, I never would have used it.

(**CLARE** *sits and silently ties the shoe.* **THEY** *watch.*)

JEREMY. I can't send this shoe.

I just can't.

Clare. It's yours.

(**CLARE** *walks over to* **JEREMY** *and gives him a long hug.* **SHE** *takes his hand and leads him back to the painting she's been working on*)

(**JEREMY** *follows her.* **HE** *looks at her painting.*)

JEREMY. Is that your sister?

CLARE. Yeah. That's Beth.

JEREMY. Clare? You realize, I'm looking at your painting.

CLARE. Yes. I do.

JEREMY. That's ok with you?

CLARE. Yeah. You're not just anyone.

(**JEREMY** *kisses her forehead and then moves out of the scene, downstage. Lights dim.* **HE** *stays lit as do the hanging photographs of the three shoes.*)

JEREMY. I sent three photographs and two shoes to New York. I explained why the third shoe was missing. I haven't heard from them yet. At this point, it really doesn't matter.

(Pause)

I found out what I wanted to know.

(Pause)

Now, when I see a shoe on the highway, I think of Clare and her sister.

I think of all the shoes, all the stories. And I feel a kind of connection.

(Pause)

We're all in this together and yet we're very much alone...

PROMETHEUS BOUND

Joseph Fisher
Drama / 3m, 2f

Based on the ancient Greek drama, Prometheus is chained to a mountain on the edge of the world as punishment for disobeying the god Zeus, condemned to see a future of violence, revenge, and destruction. As he is visited by his family, his friends, and his torturer, he attempts to understand the hidden truths of the universe and the true nature of the Gods.

Please visit our website **bakersplays.com**
for complete descriptions and licensing information

Kinda' like the shoes along the highway, right?
I'm still figuring it all out.

(Pause)

It might take me awhile.

(Blackout)

THE END

PROPS

A paper bag
6 shoes (only one of each shoe; one shoe MUST be a child's tennis shoe with shoelaces)
Photos of the shoes
3 poster-sized photos of three of the shoes on the side of the road (one of these posters MUST be of the child's tennis shoe)
An old 35 MM camera with a strap to hang around Jeremy's neck
Earphones/Ipods for Lenore and Norbert
A large garbage can
Purse with a mirror
CD player, easel
Large painting canvas
1 paint brush and a palette with paint
Clipboard for Hightower
4 stools, 3 of which double as pedestals in the museum scene
A large cardboard box

SOUND

Car motor
Large truck and loud truck horn
Police siren
School bell
Classical music for museum scene
Current music for the CD in the last scene

www.ingramcontent.com/pod-product-compliance
Lightning Source LLC
Chambersburg PA
CBHW071847290426
44109CB00017B/1963